SEALS

by Josh Gregory

Children's Press®

An Imprint of Scholastic Inc.
New York   Toronto   London   Auckland   Sydney
Mexico City   New Delhi   Hong Kong
Danbury, Connecticut

Content Consultant
Dr. Stephen S. Ditchkoff
Professor of Wildlife Sciences
Auburn University
Auburn, Alabama

Photographs ©: Alamy Images: 36 (Chronicle), 39 (Global Warming Images); Dreamstime: 2 background, 3 background, 44 background, 45 background (He Yujun), 2 foreground, 3 foreground, 40, 41, 49 (Jaymudaliar), 8, 9 (Ongm), 12, 13 (Staphy), 14, 15 (Steven Prorak), 22, 23 (Xvaldes); Getty Images: 4, 5 background, 20, 21 (Alastair Pollock Photography), 24, 25 (David Yarrow Photography), 5 top, 16, 17, 18, 19 (Doug Allan); iStockphoto/4kodiak: 26, 27; Shutterstock, Inc./Eric Isselee: 1, 32, 33; Superstock, Inc.: 6, 7 (Animals Animals), 10, 11 (Biosphoto), cover (imagebroker.net), 5 bottom, 31 (Peter Barritt), 34, 35 (Steven Kazlowski); Thinkstock/David Jones: 28, 29.

Map by Bob Italiano

Library of Congress Cataloging-in-Publication Data
Gregory, Josh, author.
  Seals / by Josh Gregory.
    pages cm. — (Nature's children)
  Audience: Ages 9–12.
  Audience: Grades 4 to 6.
  Includes bibliographical references and index.
  ISBN 978-0-531-20666-9 (lib. bdg.) —
  ISBN 978-0-531-21659-0 (pbk.)
  1. Seals (Animals)—Juvenile literature. I. Title. II. Series: Nature's children (New York, N.Y.)
  QL737.P64G74 2015
  599.79—dc23   2014001512

Printed in China 62
SCHOLASTIC, CHILDREN'S PRESS, and associated logos are trademarks and/or registered trademarks of Scholastic Inc.

1 2 3 4 5 6 7 8 9 10 R 24 23 22 21 20 19 18 17 16 15

Seals

Class	Mammalia
Order	Carnivora
Families	Phocidae and Otariidae
Genera	13 Phocidae and 7 Otariidae
Species	19 Phocidae and 16 Otariidae
World distribution	Coastal areas in most of the world's oceans; certain Phocidae species are found in lakes
Habitats	Mostly shallow coastal waters, though some species are found in lakes or farther out to sea
Distinctive physical characteristics	Long, round body that is wide at the middle; two front flippers and two hind flippers used for swimming and movement on land; short, whiskered snout; Otariidae species have visible ears, while Phocidae species do not
Habits	All species breed on land; most are social and form large groups at breeding seasons; some species form harems consisting of one male and several females, with the males defending their mates from rivals; excellent swimmers and divers; spend most of their time in the water; coastal species tend to stay in one area; those that live farther out to sea frequently migrate long distances
Diet	Mostly fish; some species eat mollusks, crustaceans, and invertebrates; leopard seals eat penguins and other birds

SEALS

Contents

6 CHAPTER 1
Coastal Hunters

14 CHAPTER 2
On Land and at Sea

26 CHAPTER 3
Seal Socialization

33 CHAPTER 4
Then and Now

37 CHAPTER 5
Sharing Space with Seals

42 Words to Know

44 Habitat Map

46 Find Out More

47 Index

48 About the Author

Coastal Hunters

Along the coast of Northern California, the waters of the Pacific Ocean look calm and pleasant. Waves crash softly on the shoreline as the sun begins to set. Far beneath the surface, however, the mood is anything but calm. A large male elephant seal is jetting upward through the ocean in search of prey. The seal has been hunting hour after hour for weeks on end. During this entire time, the seal has repeatedly swum back and forth from the surface to the ocean floor without once pausing to rest.

On this trip, the elephant seal has caught sight of a small shark swimming above. The shark is unaware of the dangerous hunter below. The seal flaps its powerful rear flippers from side to side, propelling its sleek body toward the shark. In just seconds, it has reached its prey. The seal bites down and begins to eat. Another successful dive.

An elephant seal can hold its breath for up to two hours.

A Seal's Shape

There are 35 different species of seals. While each is different from the others in some ways, all seals share the same basic body shape. A seal's body is round and wide at the middle. It gets smaller toward the animal's head and hind limbs. Seals each have four wide, flat limbs called flippers. Two are located near the front end of the seal's body. The other two are near the hind end.

Seals vary widely in size. The largest species is the elephant seal, which lives mainly along the west coast of North and South America. This huge mammal can grow to be 21 feet (6.4 meters) long and weigh up to 8,150 pounds (3,697 kilograms). That is about as heavy as two cars! The smallest seal species is the Baikal seal. It is found in only one lake in Russia. It grows to lengths of 3.6 to 4.6 feet (1.1 to 1.4 m) and weighs between 110 and 290 pounds (50 and 132 kg).

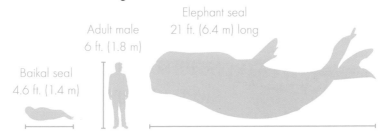

Baikal seal
4.6 ft. (1.4 m)

Adult male
6 ft. (1.8 m)

Elephant seal
21 ft. (6.4 m) long

Baikal seals are around the same weight as many humans.

Two Families

The 35 seal species are divided into two families. The family Phocidae consists of animals that are known as true seals. They are also known as earless seals. That doesn't mean they are truly earless, however. Instead, they have a very small hole on either side of the head, where ears would stick out on most other mammals.

The family Otariidae is made up of eared seals. Unlike their "earless" cousins, these seals have earflaps that stick out from the sides of their heads. They also have longer front flippers and more fur on their bodies than earless seals do. Eared seals can be divided into two categories: fur seals and sea lions. Fur seals generally have thicker coats of fur than sea lions. They also tend to have the longest front flippers of all seal species.

FUN FACT! Seals sometimes sleep underwater.

Seals in the Phocidae family are born (the young seal is on the left) without visible earflaps.

Around the World

Seals can be found in aquatic habitats throughout much of the world. Most species prefer to live in shallow coastal waters of the world's oceans. However, some types of seals swim farther out into the ocean than others do. Other seal species are found swimming in inland lakes. Many species live in some of the world's coldest waters, in the Arctic and Antarctic regions near the North and South Poles.

Earless seals are most common in the Northern Hemisphere. They are found in all of the world's oceans. Eared seals tend to live in the Southern Hemisphere. They can be found along the coasts of North and South America, Asia, and Africa. They also live along parts of Australia and New Zealand, as well as many small islands.

Fur seals rest on Adelaide Island off the coast of Antarctica.

CHAPTER 2

On Land and at Sea

All seals are **carnivores**. They have a diet that consists entirely of other animals. Because they vary so much in size and live in many different parts of the world, each seal species has a slightly different diet. Most seals eat various kinds of fish. Some eat cephalopods, which are squids, octopuses, and other similar animals. Crustaceans, which include animals such as shrimp and lobster, are also on the menu for many seal species.

Some seals have diets that stand out from those of their relatives. Certain types of earless seals eat tiny animals known as plankton. One species, the leopard seal, has the most unusual diet of all. Unlike any other seal, this Antarctic species commonly feeds on **warm-blooded** animals. Its main prey are penguins and other seabirds. However, this vicious hunter also eats smaller, younger seals, including those of its own species.

Catching dinner is not always easy for seals. It often requires a chase and a quick snatch.

Prowling for Prey

Most seal species hunt for prey by diving. Seals can zip in and snatch unsuspecting prey before the target has a chance to get away. Because different species have different diets, some seals have special hunting methods. For example, the crabeater seal is a filter feeder. As it swims through groups of plankton, it sucks water into its mouth. The tiny plankton stick to the seal's teeth, which are covered in small points. The seal then releases the water from its mouth and swallows the plankton left behind. Leopard seals hunt penguins by hiding beneath the edges of floating ice. When a penguin dives into the water, the seal is waiting to snatch it.

Seals do not chew their food. If prey is small enough, the seal swallows it whole. If the prey is larger, the seal uses its sharp teeth to tear off chunks or shreds. It can also use its teeth to crack open the shells of crustaceans.

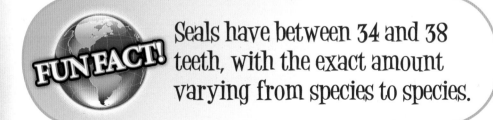

FUN FACT! Seals have between 34 and 38 teeth, with the exact amount varying from species to species.

A leopard seal can take a penguin by surprise as the bird dives into the water.

A Seal's Senses

Seals rely on their senses to find and track prey and avoid threats. In general, they have good vision and hearing. Seals can usually see well in both light and dark conditions, whether they are on a sunny beach or in the dark depths of the ocean. A seal's hearing is about as good as a human's is when it is on land. However, this sense becomes much stronger underwater. Some seals have a range of hearing more than three times greater than humans have underwater.

Seals also rely heavily on their sense of touch when they are underwater. The long whiskers on a seal's face are very sensitive. They can feel even the smallest movements in the water. As fish and other sea animals swim, they leave behind trails of movement in the water. A seal's whiskers can detect these trails from animals that passed by more than half a minute earlier. This allows the seal to track prey and avoid **predators**.

Many of a seal's senses are most effective underwater, where it uses them to hunt.

Sleek Swimmers

The sleek shape of a seal's body makes it very good at jetting through the water. Earless seals push themselves forward by moving their hind flippers back and forth. They use their front flippers to steer. Eared seals use their long front flippers like oars to pull their bodies through the water.

In general, seals can remain underwater for about 20 to 30 minutes before returning to the surface for air. This allows them to travel to depths of between 500 to 650 feet (150 to 200 m). Some species are able to go even deeper. The Weddell seal has been known to hold its breath for up to 73 minutes at a time. This allows it to reach depths of around 2,000 feet (600 m)!

Water is very cold far below the surface of the ocean, especially in the Arctic and Antarctic. Seals have thick layers of blubber beneath their skin. This helps to keep them warm as they swim through the icy water.

Seals can swim very fast and change direction quickly and easily.

Crawling Ashore

All seals spend at least some of their time on land. Earless species tend to spend much less time ashore than their eared cousins. Some species, such as the elephant seal, might spend as little as 10 percent of their lives out of the water.

Earless seals are very awkward when they move around on land. Their hind flippers point backward and cannot bend to go under the seal's body. As a result, these seals can move on land only by pulling themselves with their front flippers or wriggling their bodies a little like a caterpillar does. Despite this, they are still fairly quick on land. Some species can move even faster than a human!

Eared seals have a much easier time moving around on land. They can bend their rear flippers up beneath their bodies. This allows them to "walk" on all four limbs, almost as if they had legs.

An Australian sea lion "walks" along the beach on Kangaroo Island.

Protection from Predators

While seals are powerful hunters, they are not always at the top of the food chain. This means there are other predators that would love to make a meal of a seal. Throughout the Arctic, fierce polar bears rely on seals as a major part of their diet. Ringed seals are especially vulnerable to polar bear attacks, as the two animals' habitats overlap. At sea, seals must stay on the lookout for the deadly killer whale, also known as the orca. Some large shark species are known to eat seals, too.

A seal's main defense is its incredible swimming abilities. While seals are not quite as fast as some predators, such as killer whales, they are more agile. This means they can make quick turns to evade an attack. Some larger seal species, such as the elephant seal, are powerful enough to fight back using their teeth.

A seal's great agility in the water can make it difficult to catch, even for a great white shark.

CHAPTER 3

Seal Socialization

Seals are usually very social animals. However, the exact nature of their interactions varies from species to species. Earless seal species often form pairs or small groups. Eared seals, especially sea lions, are generally even more social. When they are on land, they sometimes form massive groups of up to 1,500 seals. These groups are known as herds. Herd members often lie piled up on top of one another on beaches.

Seals can communicate with one another using barks, growls, yelps, and other sounds. The exact sounds a seal makes depends on its species. Sea lions tend to make a lot of noise as they socialize in their herds. Earless seals tend to use soft sounds. Some species, such as the harbor seal, do not make much noise on land. Instead, they use sounds to communicate while they are underwater.

A herd of sea lions sun themselves on a rocky coast.

Mating Season

Once a year, seals have a **mating** season. The season happens at different times for different seal species. However, all species return to land for mating season, regardless of how much time they normally spend ashore.

Some seal species are **monogamous**. They form pairs and only mate with each other. Others, including all of the fur seals, form groups called harems. A harem consists of a single male seal and several females. Harem sizes change from species to species. For example, an elephant seal harem might have up to 40 females, while a gray seal harem has 10 or fewer. The male in a harem mates with all of the females. He also defends his harem from rivals. When another male approaches, the harem's male might roar or show off his teeth. If the rival does not back down, the two males clash in a bloody battle.

Male elephant seals fight to protect their harems from predators and from other males.

Playful Pups

Around 11 months after mating, seal mothers return to land. There they give birth to their **pups**. Just a few days later, they are ready to mate once again.

Seals almost always give birth to just one pup each year. Twins are possible in rare instances. Newborn pups have the same body shape as adults but are much smaller. They might also have different coloring or more fur than adults. A pup is able to move around on land as soon as it is born. It survives by drinking milk from its mother. This milk is rich in fat and other nutrients. It helps the pup grow quickly and develop blubber.

As the pup grows older, it learns to swim and catch prey. Some species are able to survive on their own after just a few weeks. Others continue **nursing** for more than a year after birth.

Antarctic fur pups are born with thick, brownish-black fur.

CHAPTER 4

Then and Now

Seals are part of a group of animals known as pinnipeds. The word *pinniped* comes from the Latin words for "feather foot." Pinnipeds were given this name because their flippers are shaped somewhat like the wings of a bird. Experts believe that the pinnipeds' earliest **ancestors** were bearlike animals that lived sometime between 34 million and 23 million years ago. These animals probably lived on land. The first sea-dwelling animals similar to today's pinnipeds appeared roughly 27 million to 25 million years ago. Most ancient species are **extinct** today. Scientists have learned about them by studying **fossils**.

Since then, new species have developed as others disappeared. Scientists organize today's earless seals into 13 **genera**. They further separate those genera into 19 species. Modern eared seals are divided into seven genera, made up of 16 species.

Pinnipeds earned their name from the winglike shape of their feet.

Tusked Cousins

In addition to both earless and eared seals, the pinniped suborder includes the walrus. This huge mammal can reach lengths of up to 12 feet (3.7 m) and weigh up to 3,700 pounds (1,678 kg). Walruses are found mainly in the icy shores of the Arctic Circle. Like seals, walruses have long, round bodies and four flippers. They also spend time both on land and in the water.

The most obvious difference between walruses and their seal relatives is the two long tusks that stick out of their mouths. Each tusk can be up to 3 feet (0.9 m) long! The tusks are used mainly to fight off rivals and attract mates.

Walruses eat mostly small animals such as clams and mussels. Like seals, they use their sensitive whiskers to detect the movement of prey in the dark areas near the ocean floor. On occasion, walruses hunt larger prey, including fish and even small seals.

Both male and female walruses have tusks.

CHAPTER 5

Sharing Space with Seals

Seals face many dangers in their wild habitats. However, the biggest threats of all do not come from natural predators or harsh living conditions, but from human activities. Throughout history, humans have purposely killed seals for many reasons. In the 1800s, seals were hunted for their skin, blubber, and meat. At its peak, the seal hunting industry killed as many as 687,000 seals per year. Some species, such as the elephant seal, came close to extinction. In the 1900s, fishermen often killed seals because they thought the seals were reducing the amount of fish that were available to catch. Seal hunting continues today. However, there are now laws and regulations in place to limit the number of seals that are killed and to prevent hunters from killing baby seals.

Many seals are also killed accidentally. Sometimes boats and ships hit them. Other times, seals get caught in fishing nets and lines. They cannot escape, and they are often seriously injured.

Serious overhunting of seals and their relatives occurred during the 19th and 20th centuries.

Problems with Pollution

Seals also suffer from the damage that humans have caused to the environment. One major problem for seals and other marine life in recent decades has been oil spills. Humans often drill for oil on the ocean floor. They also use ships to transport oil. When something goes wrong with these operations, huge amounts of oil can leak into the water.

Oil spills cause many problems for seals. When seals come to the surface of oily water to breathe, they inhale dangerous vapors that can damage their lungs. Oil can also damage seals' eyes, and baby seals might accidentally consume oil from their mothers' bodies while nursing. Fur seals face even bigger problems. When their fur is clean, it keeps water from touching their skin. This keeps the seals warm in cold water. Oily fur allows water to seep through. As a result, the seals can get very cold and die.

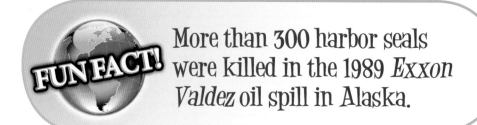

FUN FACT! More than 300 harbor seals were killed in the 1989 *Exxon Valdez* oil spill in Alaska.

Oil floats on top of ocean waters and covers seals as they surface.

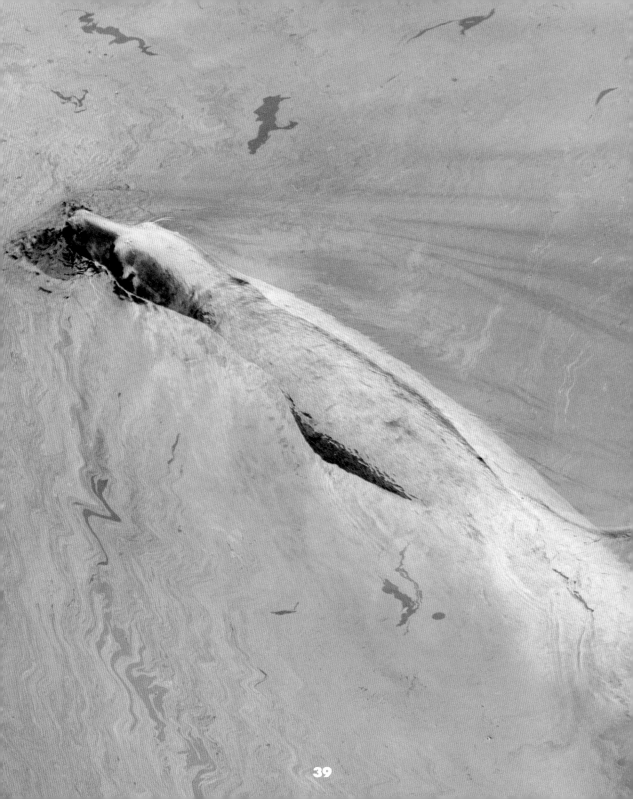

Disappearing Homes

Climate change is another problem for many seals. Some seals, such as the harp seal, live in areas where there is not much land. Instead, they rely on huge chunks of floating ice for space to mate and raise pups. As global temperatures increase, much of this ice is beginning to melt away. In addition, some of the ice that remains has become much thinner. It can break apart, separating pups from their mothers. Falling ice can kill the young pups. Less ice also leaves fewer places for young seals to rest when making long journeys through the water. They can become exhausted and drown.

By fighting the effects of climate change and pollution and by regulating hunting, we can ensure that seals continue to thrive in years to come. These remarkable animals deserve a long future of swimming and diving through the world's waters.

Global warming can lead to serious problems for seals who depend on the ice for survival.

Words to Know

ancestors (AN-ses-turz) — ancient animal species that are related to modern species

blubber (BLUH-bur) — the layer of fat under the skin of a whale, seal, or other large marine mammal

carnivores (KAHR-nuh-vorz) — animals that eat mostly meat

climate change (KLYE-mut CHAYNJ) — global warming and other changes in the weather and weather patterns that are happening because of human activity

extinct (ik-STINGKT) — no longer found alive

families (FAM-uh-leez) — groups of living things that are related to each other

fossils (FAH-suhlz) — bones, shells, or other traces of an animal or plant from thousands or millions of years ago, preserved as rock

genera (JEH-nuh-ruh) — groups of related plants or animals that are larger than a species but smaller than a family

habitats (HAB-uh-tats) — the places where an animal or plant is usually found

hemisphere (HEM-uh-sfeer) — one-half of Earth

mammal (MAM-uhl) — a warm-blooded animal that has hair or fur and usually gives birth to live babies; female mammals produce milk to feed their young

mating (MAY-ting) — joining with another animal to reproduce

monogamous (muh-NAH-guh-muhs) — having only one mate

nursing (NUR-sing) — consuming milk produced by the mother

predators (PRED-uh-turz) — animals that live by hunting other animals for food

prey (PRAY) — an animal that's hunted by another animal for food

pups (PUPS) — the young of various animals

species (SPEE-sheez) — one of the groups into which animals and plants of the same genus are divided; members of the same species can mate and have offspring

suborder (SUB-or-dur) — a group of related plants or animals that is bigger than a family and smaller than an order

warm-blooded (WORM-BLUHD-id) — describing animals whose body temperature stays about the same, even if the temperature around them is very hot or very cold

Habitat Map

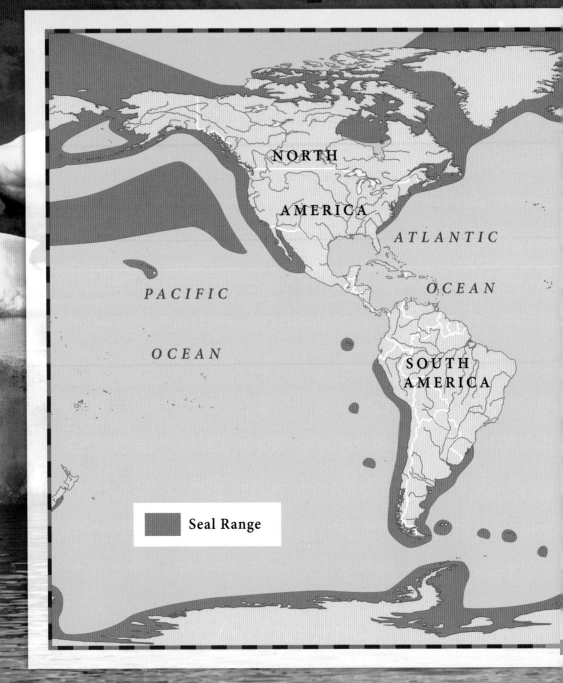

NORTH AMERICA

ATLANTIC

OCEAN

PACIFIC

OCEAN

SOUTH AMERICA

Seal Range

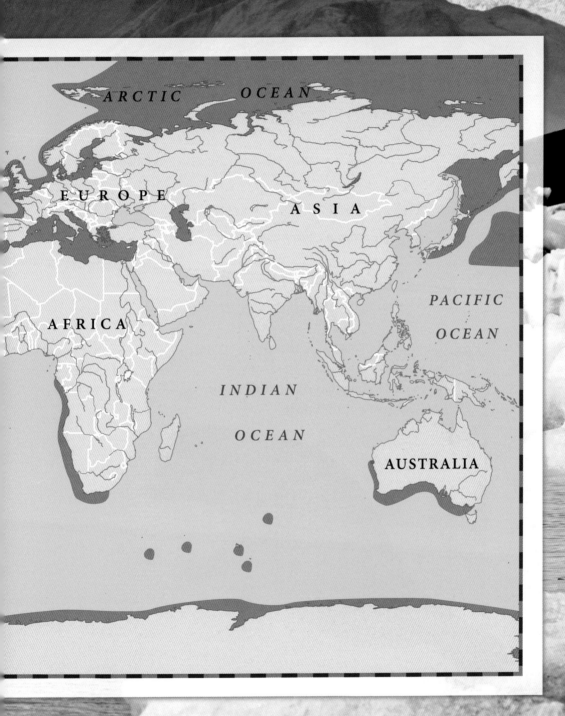

ARCTIC OCEAN

EUROPE

ASIA

AFRICA

PACIFIC OCEAN

INDIAN

OCEAN

AUSTRALIA

Find Out More

Books

Gallagher, Debbie. *Seals and Sea Lions*. New York: Marshall Cavendish Benchmark, 2010.

Markle, Sandra. *Leopard Seals*. Minneapolis: Lerner Publications, 2010.

Throp, Claire. *Seals*. Chicago: Heinemann Library, 2013.

Visit this Scholastic Web site for more information on seals:
www.factsfornow.scholastic.com
Enter the keyword **Seals**

Index

Page numbers in *italics* indicate a photograph or map.

Adelaide Island, *12*
ancient species, 33

babies. *See* pups.
Baikal seals, *8*, 9
blubber, 21, 30, 37

carnivores, 14
cephalopods, 14
climate change, *40*, 41
colors, 30, *31*
communication, 26, 29
conservation, 37, 41
crabeater seals, 17
crustaceans, 14, 17

defenses, *24*, 25, *28*, 29, 34
diving, 17

eared seals, 10, 13, 21, 22, 26, 33
earless seals, 10, *11*, 13, 14, 21, 22, 26, 33
elephant seals, 6, *7*, 9, 22, 25, *28*, 29, 37
extinction, 33, 37

females, 29, 30, *35*, 41
flippers, 6, 9, 10, 21, 22, *32*, 33, 34
food. *See* milk; prey.
fossils, 33
fur, 10, 30, *31*, 38

fur seals, 10, *12*, 29, *31*, 38

genera, 33

habitats, 6, 9, *12*, 13, *23*, 25, 34, 37, 38
harbor seals, 26, 38
harems, *28*, 29
harp seals, 41
herds, 26, *27*
hunting, 6, *15*, *16*, 17, 18, *19*, 25, 30, 34, *36*, 37, 41

Kangaroo Island, *23*
killer whales, 25

lengths, 9, *9*, 10, 34
leopard seals, 14, *16*, 17

males, 6, *28*, 29, *35*
mating, 29, 30, 34, 41
meat, 37
milk, 30, 38
monogamy, 29

oil spills, 38, *39*
Otariidae family, 10

people, 18, *36*, 37, 38
Phocidae family, 10, *11*
pinnipeds, *32*, 33, 34
plankton, 14, 17

(Index continued)

polar bears, 25
predators, 6, 18, *24*, 25, *36*, 37
prey, 6, 14, *15*, *16*, 17, 18, 30, 34
pups, 30, *31*, 38, 41

ringed seals, 25

sea lions, 10, *23*, 26, *27*
senses, 18, *19*
shapes, 9, 21, 30, *32*, 33, 34
sharks, 6, *24*, 25
sizes, *8*, 9, *9*, 14, 29, 34
skin, 21, 37, 38
social interaction, 26
species, 9, 10, 13, 14, 17, 21, 22, 25, 26, 29, 30, 33, 37
speeds, *20*, 22, 25

swimming, 6, *7*, 13, 17, 18, *19*, *20*, 21, *24*, 25, 26, 30, 38, *39*

teeth, 17, 25, 29
temperatures, 13, 21, 38, 41
true seals, 10
tusks, 34, *35*

walking, 22, *23*
walruses, 34, *35*
Weddell seals, 21
weight, *8*, 9, 34
whiskers, 18, 34

About the Author

Josh Gregory writes and edits books for kids. He lives in Chicago, Illinois.